NATIONAL GEOGRAPHIC INVESTIGATES NATIONAL GEOGRAPHIC INVESTIGATES NATIONAL GEOGRAPHIC INVESTIGATES NATIONAL GEOGRAPHIC INVESTIGATES NATIONAL GEOGRAPHIC INVESTIGATES NATIONAL GEOGRAPHIC INVESTIGATES NATIONAL GEOGRAPHIC INVESTIGATES NATIONAL GEOGRAPHIC INVESTIGATES NATIONAL GEOGRAPHIC INVESTIGATES NATIONAL GEOGRAPHIC INVESTIGATES NATIONAL GEOGRAPHIC

Ancient
Aztec

Archaeology Unlocks the Secrets of Mexico's Past

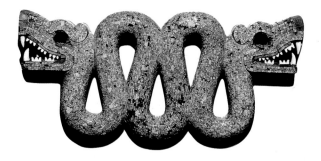

Ancient
Aztec

Archaeology Unlocks the Secrets of Mexico's Past

By Tim Cooke

Elizabeth Graham, Consultant

NATIONAL
GEOGRAPHIC

Washington, DC

Contents

< This reconstruction of the Aztec calendar stone has been painted to show how it may
have appeared. The stone divided history into a series of ages, ruled by the gods.

◀ The so-called Temple of the Chimneys in Zempoala, Veracruz, is named for the columns on the top. They are not actually chimneys at all.

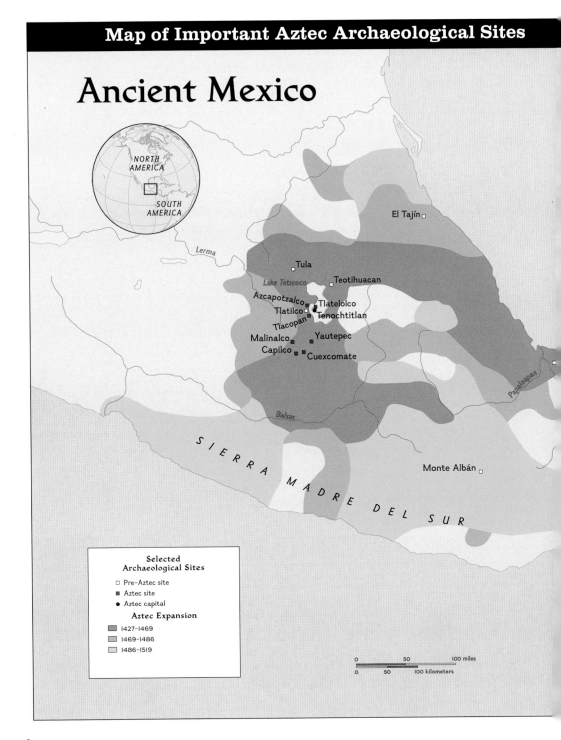

Map of Important Aztec Archaeological Sites

Ancient Mexico

NORTH AMERICA

SOUTH AMERICA

El Tajín

Lerma

Tula

Lake Tetzcoco

Teotihuacan

Azcapotzalco
Tlatilco · Tlatelolco
Tlacopan · Tenochtitlan

Malinalco · Yautepec
Capilco · Cuexcomate

Balsas

SIERRA MADRE DEL SUR

Monte Albán

Papaloapan

Selected Archaeological Sites

□ Pre-Aztec site
■ Aztec site
● Aztec capital

Aztec Expansion

1427–1469
1469–1486
1486–1519

0   50   100 miles
0   50   100 kilometers

8

of Mexico

Usumacinta

La Venta

FIC

AN

For many years, Aztec civilization was known to us largely through written accounts. Spanish soldiers and officials wrote about their encounters, and Spanish monks recorded information on Aztec culture. The Aztecs themselves kept records as rulers of a great empire, but they also wrote during the Spanish conquest about loss and the passing of their cherished way of life. Because so many Spanish colonial towns and cities were built over Aztec towns and cities, archaeological information on Aztec life has long been buried.

But things are changing these days. Excavations such as the work carried out by archaeologists uncovering the Templo Mayor in Mexico City are revealing spectacular remains of Aztec buildings and sculptures. Aztec townspeople and village dwellers are also springing to life through excavations of communities that tell us about families, large and small, and their everyday lives.

It is an exciting time, full of new discoveries for archaeologists, although the many descendents of the Aztec living throughout Mexico are probably just saying, "Told you so."

Elizabeth Graham
London, 2007

Central Mexico

The Olmec

ca 1200 – 400 B.C.

The Olmec were the founders of the first great civilization of Mesoamerica. Their cities appeared in the Gulf Coast region of Mexico beginning in the second millennium B.C. The Olmec were master sculptors of both huge monumental pieces weighing several tons and small objects that could fit in the hand. Olmec monumental architecture, their religion, calendar, and writing system influenced all later Mesoamerican cultures. As a result, their civilization is seen as the "mother culture" of the region.

Teotihuacan

ca 150 B.C. – A.D. 750

For around 900 years Teotihuacan was a large city covering 8 square miles (20 sq km) with 100,000–200,000 inhabitants. It was the largest city in the Americas at the time. Teotihuacan had a wide influence throughout Mesoamerica. It was a thriving trade center, where many crafts were produced. The city was mysteriously abandoned in the 8th century.

< This pottery figure was made by an Olmec craft worker over 3,000 years ago.

> A Toltec column shows the god Quetzalcoatl peeking out of the jaws of a serpent. Quetzalcoatl was also an important god for the Aztec.

Timeline of Mexican History

A.D. 500

1000

Olmec
1200–400 B.C.

ca 600
Teotithuacan at the height of its power and influence

ca 900
Toltec capital
Tula founded

ca 1100
Aztec begin search for a new homeland

ca 1200 Aztec arrive in the Valley of Mexic

Teotihuacan 150 B.C.–A.D. 750

Toltec 950–1150

< This mask was found at Teotihuacan. It may have been placed on top of a stake and used in religious ceremonies.

e Toltec

950–1150

r the fall of Teotihuacan,
y small city-states
peted for power in
ral Mexico. The Toltec
ually came to
inate. Their capital was
la, around 35 miles
h of Tenochtitlan. The
c practiced human
fice on a large scale
had a warrior culture.
e 12th century their
les were destroyed and
ity abandoned.

The Aztec Empire

ca 1430 – 1521

The Aztec arrived in central Mexico from the north in the 12th century. They slowly built up their strength. From their capital Tenochtitlan, they expanded to create a large empire beginning in the mid–15th century with the help of their allies. At the height of its power, the empire controlled an area of 116,000 square miles (300,000 sq km) and collected tribute from millions of people.

< This Aztec breastplate made of gold and turquoise was created in the form of a shield pierced by arrows.

1500

1440 Moctezuma I begins 28-year reign in Tenochtitlan

434 Triple Alliance takes control of the of Mexico

1502 Moctezuma II begins his rule. The Aztec empire is at its peak

2000

1821 Mexican independence

1519 Cortés lands in Mexico on April 21, enters Tenochtitlan on November 8

1520 Moctezuma II dies

1521 Siege of Tenochtitlan. Spanish victory results in the fall of the empire

■ Aztec Empire ca 1430–1521

Yesterday Comes Alive

CHAPTER 1

How do we learn what we know about the past?

Mexico City's main square, the Zocalo, does not look like a promising site for finding ancient ruins or remains. Traffic snarls the streets around one of the largest city centers in the world. It is covered in concrete and lined by grand buildings. For nearly 500 years, the square has been the heart of the capital and the country. The Spanish built the city right on top of the Aztec capital Tenochtitlan, covering all signs of the people who lived there before them.

But those signs are reappearing. Construction projects have yielded many finds over the last two

< Mexican archaeologists examine the site in the Zocalo, Mexico City's main square, where one of 14 Aztec stone carvings was discovered in January 2005.

13

centuries, from statues to the ruins of a great temple. The temple, the Templo Mayor, once stood at the heart of the largest empire ever seen in Mesoamerica. The Aztec Empire was at its height in the 15th and early 16th centuries. Today most of Tenochtitlan lies beneath modern Mexico City. But even now, new finds sometimes come to light that change what we know about the Aztec.

Exciting discovery

In October 2006 workers at the Templo Mayor found part of a stone block carved by the Aztec more than 500 years earlier. As experts uncovered the stone, they came to realize its importance. At 46 square feet (14 sq m) and weighing 13.6 tons (12.4 tonnes), it was the largest single Aztec block ever found. It had elaborate carvings that the experts recognized as Tlaltecuhtli, one of the chief Aztec gods There was an altar nearby. The block might have been a giant idol, worshiped during religious ceremonies.

The block alone was an exciting discovery—and there might be still more to come. Experts believe that it might hide the entrance to a ruined temple. Clearing the stone will take months of careful work. Archaeologists have to work like detectives at a crime scene: They record not just what they find but also exactly where they find it. Every piece of information might be vital, even if it doesn't appear to be important at first glance.

Archaeologists in Mexico are used to careful work. Spectacular finds are rare. Most Aztec cities are buried

▼ **Eduardo Matos Moctezuma, who leads the excavations at the Templo Mayor in Mexico City, talks to the press about the discovery of the huge carved image of a blood-drinking Aztec god in October 2006.**

< A gold breastplate in the form of the fire god, Xiuhtecuhtli. Much Aztec gold was shipped to Spain, often after being melted down.

find out more about the relationships between the Aztec and other peoples of the time, and with their descendants. Others concentrate on Aztec art, such as statues or jewelry.

The Aztec had no alphabet or writing system as we know it. They relied on word of mouth to pass information from generation to generation. They also created records known as *codices* (singular: *codex*). These were sheets of deerskin or tree bark, folded like books. They contained

eneath later cities and are difficult to xcavate. Rural sites may yield new nformation, but the process is slow. xperts move ahead in small steps ather than great leaps. They have to iece together information from shards f pottery, or the layout of a building.

ictorial records

Iany archaeologists who study the ztec rarely leave their offices or boratories. Instead of digging up ncient sites, they study languages to

The front page of the Codex Mendoza shows an gle in a cactus at the site of Tenochtitlan, rrounded by the leaders of the Aztec tribes who unded the city.

What's in a name?

The term "Aztec" was first used by an 18th-century explorer and became popular in the 19th century. It means "people of Aztlan," which refers to the mythical homeland of the Aztec. But in fact the empire was made up of different groups.

The people of Tenochtitlan, for example, called themselves Tenochca, Mexica, or Mexica-Colhua. The empire (which they called the Triple Alliance) also contained the Acolhua of Texcoco, the Tepanec of Azcapotzalco, the Chalca, Xochimilca, Tlahuica, and other groups. So in many ways the name Aztec is misleading. Because it is the name that most people know, experts still use it. But it is important to remember that it is a kind of shorthand, and that it actually refers to all the peoples of the empire.

V **This turquoise-mosaic handle once held a knife blade, which has now been lost. It is so well made that it may have had a special purpose—perhaps even the ritual killing of prisoners.**

drawn symbols, called *glyphs*, that stood for specific things, such as dates or place-names. They also illustrated myths and legends and gods. After the Spanish conquered the Aztec in 1521, they destroyed most codices because they connected them with Aztec religion, which they wanted to replace with Christianity. Very few preconquest codices survive.

These sources have been lost, but experts can still study other written sources. They were created after the fall of the empire and kept in libraries in Mexico or in Europe. Some accounts of the Aztec were written by the Spanish conquerors, who saw the empire at its peak. Later, Spanish monks and scholars got Aztec artists to help them record Aztec language, history, and culture. They made books that still give us a window into the Aztec world.

Aztec wonders

As we will see, archaeology confirms many of the various written accounts. They portray an organized society where most people lived in cities. Some citizens had duties as government officials, priests, or warriors. The Aztec had a system of schools and medical knowledge that was far better than that of the Spaniards.

The Spanish conquerors were amazed by

Tenochtitlan. As you'll discover in chapter 3, its ruins have revealed the high level of Aztec building skill.

At the same time, the conquerors were shocked by the religious rituals of the Aztec. The Spaniards described ceremonies in which Aztec priests led thousands of war captives up pyramids to cut out their hearts. Archaeologists are trying to understand why the priests thought killing was important. In chapter 4 you can explore the religious beliefs of the Aztec.

Busy cities

When the Aztec arrived in central Mexico in the 12th century, the area had already seen the rise and fall of rich civilizations. As you'll find out in chapter 2, archaeologists are still discovering more about the peoples that came before the Aztec. The Aztec founded their capital Tenochtitlan in 1325, but their empire took much longer to build. Their long rise to power is investigated in chapter 5. Military strength was at the heart of the rise. But the Aztec were also skilled diplomats. They made agreements that increased their power at the expense of their neighbors.

Recently there have been exciting discoveries in a previously little-studied area of Aztec life—how ordinary people lived. In chapter 6 you'll share some of the latest investigations into everyday life in the Aztec Empire, out in the provinces far from the great centers of power.

▽ The restored temple-pyramid of Santa Cecilia Acatitlan near Tenochtitlan. Religious ceremonies including human sacrifice were performed here.

Cities of the Gods

CHAPTER 2

What do we know about people before the Aztec?

Archaeology is a relatively new science. But trying to find out about the past is as old as humanity. Everyone is curious about people who lived before them. That includes the Aztec who moved into the Valley of Mexico in the 13th century. Near Tenochtitlan, they discovered an abandoned city, overgrown with vegetation. Two stepped stone pyramids rose at either end of a wide avenue lined with stone buildings.

< Archaeologist Linda Mazan measures a skull in a burial site in Teotihuacan, an ancient abandoned city rediscovered and looted by the Aztec.

OLMEC ca 1200 – 400 B.C.

TEOTIHUACAN
ca 150 B.C.–A.D. 750

TOLTEC
ca 950 – 1150

1200 B.C.   0   A.D. 1200

Unlike modern archaeologists, the Aztec interpreted the ruins to fit their own beliefs. They called the city Teotihuacan, or "city of the gods." They named the two pyramids for the sun and the moon and called the main avenue the Street of the Dead. As archaeologists proved over 700 years later, the name was strangely accurate.

Pyramid of death

In 2006, a joint Japanese and Mexican team exploring Teotihuacan tunneled into the 140-foot-tall (43 m) Pyramid of the Moon. It was dangerous work. As they dug, they used steel beams to hold up the roofs of the tunnels so the weight of the pyramid wouldn't bring them crashing down. As they got deeper, the air became too stale to breathe. The team had to rig up pumps to bring in clean air from the outside.

The excavations showed that the pyramid had been built in seven stages, one on top of the other. As the team explored each layer, they found bones—lots of bones. At five sites lay the skeletons of eagles, wolves, pumas, and rattlesnakes—symbols of power in Mesoamerica.

There were human bones, too. In one pit, 12 bodies still had their hands bound behind their backs. Most had their heads cut off. In another grave,

▽ The Street of the Dead leads to the Pyramid of the Moon. The cutaway at right shows the different stages in which the pyramid was enlarged (1-7). The small pits inside the pyramid mark places where archaeologists have discovered bones (A-E).

You are what you eat

Scientists can find out what ancient peoples ate from their bones. Over a lifetime, what a person eats leaves a chemical pattern in his or her skeleton. English bioarchaeologist Dr. Tamsin O'Connell is interpreting these patterns to learn more about prehistoric diets.

To find out what diets create a particular pattern, O'Connell studies groups of living humans. But luckily, she does not have to study their bones. She has discovered that hair from the living provides the same chemical information as bone samples from the dead!

∧ **Ancient bones at Teotihuacan.**

guessed that the animals and people had been sacrificed during the building of the pyramid, which took 100 years, beginning in about 300 B.C. But the beliefs of the builders remain a mystery. Expedition member Leonardo López Luján said, "These offerings are like sentences, but we don't have all the words and we don't completely understand their sequence, so they're hard to read."

Mysterious fate

By A.D. 400, Teotihuacan was a great city covering 8 square miles (21 sq km). Discovery of artifacts—gems and precious metals—showed that it was a trading center. There were many workshops for craftspeople.

Teotihuacan came to a sudden end. It was abandoned about A.D. 600 and stood empty until it was discovered

∨ **This mask unearthed at Teotihuacan has ear spools and a nose pendant. These ornaments were worn by nobles.**

7 skulls lay in a grisly pile. heir owners had suffered the ame fate. Nearby lay jewelry, eads, and small pottery gures of people.

None of the ctims came from eotihuacan. Their ones and teeth ere different om others found the city, showing at they had eaten different diet. Experts

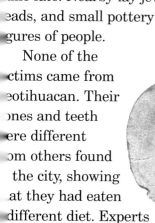

∧ Statues of warriors, known as the Atlantes, stand on top of a pyramid at Tula.

nearly 700 years later—by the Aztec. What happened to Teotihuacan is a mystery. Maybe its answer also lies buried in the Pyramid of the Moon.

Toltec splendor?

Teotihuacan was not the only ancient city the Aztec explored. About 35 miles (56 km) north of Tenochtitlan lay another abandoned city. Many experts identified it as Tula, the capital of the Toltec, who dominated central Mexico between about 950 and 1150. The Aztec took sculptures from Tula to decorate their buildings.

Ruins and artifacts reveal little about the Toltec. Some experts doubt whether the site was Tula at all. Whatever the answer, the city's end

was sudden. Its monuments were destroyed in about 1150.

Giant carvings

Centuries before Teotihuacan and Tula existed, cities thrived near the Gulf of Mexico. In 1862, a workman clearing a field at Tres Zapotes came across what he thought was an old kettle. But when his neighbors helped, they uncovered a stone head, nearly 5 feet (1.5 m) tall and weighing 8 tons (7.2 tonnes). The face had staring eyes, a flat nose, and wore what might be a helmet.

The discovery attracted scholars in the 1930s and 1940s. They found a number of urban sites nearby, which suggested a great civilization once existed in the region. In the 1950s, scientists used radiocarbon dating to find out when. All living material contains carbon. When it dies, the carbon atoms begin to decay at a steady rate. Measuring the carbon left gives an accurate date for the material.

Buried heads

The results were remarkable. A site named San Lorenzo dated from about 1200 to 900 B.C.—far earlier than any other urban culture in the Americas. The settlement was a center of the Olmec, whose culture influenced later peoples in Mesoamerica. The Aztec calendar, for example, was based on the Olmec calendar.

In 2006, experts found a stone tablet that may represent an Olmec writing system. It is carved with rows

A sacred ball game

One theory about the Olmec heads is that they show players of the sacred ball game. Throughout Mesoamerica, ball courts show that the game was played by many different peoples. Carvings show that the game involved using the elbows and knees to pass a ball through iron rings.

No one knows if the Olmec headgear really was a sports helmet, but the ball game was important everywhere. It likely had a religious meaning. Some experts argue that the losers of the game were sacrificed to the gods—but others think that it was the winners who were killed.

> Mexican archaeologist Dr. Ponciano Ortiz discovered this 3,000-year-old latex ball at the Olmec site of El Manati: it still smelled of rubber.

of 62 symbols, like modern writing. Some experts think that the tablet may be a fake. But if the Olmec really did write 3,000 years ago, that would mean some rewriting now—of the history books.

Ann Cyphers Guillén, from the National Autonomous University of Mexico, is more interested in the most famous Olmec monuments. In 1994 she unearthed a tenth giant stone head at San Lorenzo. Like the others, it had been buried. No one knows why. Maybe invaders overthrew the Olmec and buried the heads. Or maybe each head showed a real king. When he died, his monument was buried. The calm expressions of the statues do not give us any clues.

∧ This massive stone head was one of several found at the Olmec site of San Lorenzo.

CHAPTER 3

The Heart of the Empire

How do we know what Tenochtitlan was like?

There is not much to see of Tenochtitlan. The most important temples and monuments in the Aztec capital were destroyed by the Spaniards. The rest of the city was later built over during the growth of Mexico City, which today has more than 18 million residents. Most archaeological work has begun with lucky, accidental finds. But that does not mean that we do not know about the great city. In fact, we know more about it than about almost any other ancient capital.

< The Templo Mayor in the heart of Mexico City is the biggest archaeological site in the capital. The Catholic Metropolitan Cathedral rises in the background.

AZTEC 1100 – 1521

1100   1600

The building of a subway in the 1960s and 1970s produced cratefuls of artifacts. There were so many that scholars could not keep up. They had to put the objects in storage while they analyzed them all.

Colorful capital

Another important source is the accounts left by the conquistadors—conquerors—who arrived with Hernán Cortés. The visitors could not fail to be impressed. At a time when the largest city in Spain had a population of 60,000, the Aztec capital was home to about 200,000 people. Tenochtitlan was built on an island in a lake. The island covered about 4 square miles (10 sq km) and was connected to the shore by three broad causeways. The buildings rising in the sacred area in the heart of the city were colored with red, green, turquoise and yellow plaster. An aqueduct supplied the city with fresh drinking water, while countless canoes carried food and other goods from the shore to busy markets. Even the Spaniards who

∧ The Aztec built "floating gardens" in Lake Tetzcoco. They piled soil on rafts, where they planted crops and even trees. Over time, plant roots grew down through the rafts to the bottom of the lake, where they held the islands in place.

⋀ Xochimilco, just south of Mexico City, is all that remains of the "floating gardens."

had seen great cities like Rome in Italy admitted that they had never seen anything like Tenochtitlan.

A mythical journey

The city's founding was part of Aztec myth. The Spaniards reported that students learned the story at school and poets wrote about it. Artists illustrated it in codices. The story reveals much about the origins of the Aztec—but not everything.

No one knows, for example, where the Aztec came from. Aztlan, their mythical homeland, was a dry region full of cactus. It probably lay in what

is now northern Mexico or the southwestern United States. Eight tribes set out, either driven out by hostile neighbors or searching for better land.

One codex has a glyph—a picture symbol—dating the event to the early 1100s. According to the myth, the god Huitzilopochtli guided the tribes and predicted that the Aztec would settle where they found a cactus sprouting from a rock, with an eagle perching among its thorns.

After a journey that lasted several generations, the Aztec arrived at Chapultepec, "grasshopper hill," on the shores of Lake Tetzcoco. They served natives of the area—the Colhuacan—as warriors. As the Aztec grew more

⋀ This statue of Coatlicue, the chief Aztec goddess, stood in the courtyard of the Templo Mayor.

⋁ This artist's view of Tenochtitlan is based on the accounts of the first Spaniards to see the Aztec city in the middle of Lake Tetzcoco. Three long causeways connected the city to the shore.

powerful, however, the Colhuacan became alarmed and turned on their allies. The Aztec fled into the swampy lake, where they found the sign foretold by the legend and founded their city. Tenochtitlan means "place of the prickly pear cactus."

Rise to power

The eagle and the cactus appear in a codex that records the history of Tenochtitlan. It dates the founding of the city to 1325. On one page are drawings of two burning temples. They mark the defeat of the Colhuacan and Tenayuca. The Aztec overthrew the cities while serving as paid soldiers for a people called the Tepanec. In reality, though, they were building their own power.

The codex records more Aztec victories. The defeated groups acknowledged Aztec rule. They sent gold and other produce to Tenochtitlan as a form of payment called *tribute*. Victory in battle also produced captives to help build the city—and to be killed in huge numbers in its temples. In barely 200 years, the nomadic tribes had become lords of the Valley of Mexico.

Building the city

Augusto F. Molina Montes of Mexico's National School of

Digging in the city

Working in cities creates special problems for archaeologists. It is not just the challenge of being in the public eye, with visitors wanting to see what is going on. Most archaeologists enjoy having people interested in their work—as long as they keep out of the way. But ancient sites in cities are often buried. When they come to light— usually during construction—the first problem is one of access. It may be impossible to knock down buildings or excavate beneath them. That makes it difficult to get large machinery or big teams of people onto a site.

Sometimes time is the problem. Local authorities might be able to protect a site, but it is more likely that they can only halt building for a limited time. Archaeologists race to save as much as possible, taking away what they can or otherwise recording a site before it is covered up. In some cases, building plans can be changed to preserve ancient remains. Aztec ruins have been left in the basements of new buildings, for example, where the public can visit them or see them through windows.

∧ This round Aztec temple has been left exposed inside the subway station at Pino Suárez.

nthropology has studied the building f the city. When it was founded, the ztec were a small group with hostile eighbors. They likely concentrated n warfare and on growing food. It as only as their power grew that iey could attract skilled craftsmen to elp build the capital.

The builders faced problems ecause of the swampy soil. Heavy uildings sank several feet beneath the vel of the rest of the city. When that appened, the Aztec often built a new structure on top of the old one.

Architects overcame the problem by using a volcanic rock called *tezontle*, which is very light, to cut the weight of structures. Tezontle was used for the bulk of the buildings, which were then covered with a layer of hard stone such as basalt. The builders also created deep foundations. They drove piles— wooden stakes up to 33 feet (10 m) long—into the earth to make a solid base for construction. The Spaniards later used the same technique.

An ancient craft

The Aztec workers used tools that had been used for centuries by other city-builders in Mesoamerica, such as axes, hammers, and chisels made from obsidian, a hard, black stone. They bored holes with wooden drills tipped with quartz, a rock that was hard enough to wear away other stone. North of the city, workers inserted wooden wedges into cracks in rock faces. They drove the wedges in to open the cracks until a block broke away. They probably moved the blocks to the city using rollers made from tree trunks or on sleds, which they pulled with ropes. They also carried them by river on barges.

What remains

Not all of Tenochtitlan has vanished. The ruins of the old Great Temple have been excavated near the main square. At the station of Pino Suárez, subway designers left exposed a temple to the god Ehecatl found during excavations. And in the Plaza of the Three Cultures rise red-brown steps that belonged to a large temple. This was the sacred plaza of Tlatelolco. Although it is now part of Mexico City, it was originally a twin city that stood next to Tenochtitlan. Its temple was said to rival that of the capital itself.

V **This reconstruction shows the busy marketplace in Tlatelolco, next to Tenochtitlan.**

inal defeat

latelolco was the site of the last efeat of the Aztec. On the temple :eps, the Spaniards overcame the ıst Aztec leader who resisted them— uauhtemoc—on August 13, 1521. A panish colonial church rises above ıe Aztec temple steps, and today oth old buildings are surrounded by ıe modern city. The city is the third " the "three cultures" for which the ıuare is named. A plaque set up by ıe Mexican government marks the ʻent and its importance in the eation of Mexico's mixed (mestizo) eritage: "It was neither a triumph ɔr a defeat, but the painful birth of ıe mestizo people that is the Mexico today."

∧ Aztec temple steps, a Spanish church, and modern office buildings in the Plaza de las Tres Culturas (Plaza of the Three Cultures) in Mexico City.

That was not how the Aztec saw the destruction of their cities. For them, it was a defeat. The Spaniards pulled down their sacred statues and leveled the great temples. They dumped rubble into the canals. That began a process that would end in the draining of almost all of Lake Tetzcoco. In the place of Tenochtitlan and Tlatelolco, the buildings of Mexico City began to rise. An unknown Aztec poet wrote a sad poem about the capital in the Nahuatl language: "We have pounded our heads in despair against the adobe walls, for our inheritance, our city, is lost and dead."

Great Temple of Death

CHAPTER 4

What do we know about Aztec religious beliefs?

In February 1978, Mario Alberto Espejel Pérez was working the night shift, digging a trench for new power cables in Mexico City's main square. When his shovel clanged against something hard and he cleared away some dirt, he saw a stone surface decorated with carvings. Pérez knew that his discovery might be important. He remembered his teachers telling him about Aztec treasures found during the building of the subway in the 1960s. He called his boss—and his boss called the National Institute of History and

◁ These carved skulls stare out from the wall of the Templo Mayor, where the Aztec killed many thousands of prisoners.

AZTEC EMPIRE
ca 1430 – 1521

1100   1600

< The stone showing the dead Coyolxauhqui stood beside the steps of the Templo Mayor.

he had his sister beheaded and her body cut into pieces. The carving of Coyolxauhqui was an important part of rituals at the Great Temple. It was a symbol of defeat and death. Some archaeologists believe that prisoners were led past the stone on the way to their deaths.

Digging up downtown

Soon after the discovery of the stone, Eduardo Matos Moctezuma began the first proper excavations on the Great Temple itself. At first his team dug in a parking lot; when the site grew, the team knocked down nearby buildings. Working in a busy city caused some problems, mainly due to the constant traffic, but it also had advantages. Matos Moctezuma could summon all kinds of experts to the site, from city planners to soil scientists. There were many volunteers—mainly students— work and a steady stream of visitors from the National Palace, a few yards away. These political visitors helped publicize the project and make sure that it got the funds it needed.

Matos Moctezuma's team uncovered not just one but five

Anthropology. So many artifacts turn up in Mexico City that the institute has a department just to rescue them. The experts moved in—and discovered a rare treasure indeed.

A goddess in pieces

The circular stone was carved with a female body cut into pieces. The archaeologists knew that this was no ordinary woman. The Spaniards who overthrew the Aztec in the 16th century had recorded a myth about the god Huitzilopochtli and his sister, Coyolxauhqui. The pair led their people from their homeland to the site of Tenochtitlan. There Huitzilopochtli argued with his sister and their brothers. The two groups fought. When Huitzilopochtli won the battle, different temples, built one on top of the other. Different rulers, they concluded, had built new temples to prove their own glory. The temple had also been repaired often, probably because it was built on soft ground and tended to sink. The façade, or front face, had been rebuilt up to 11 times.

Twin temples

At the top of the earliest structure stood temples to the gods who were most responsible for the Aztec rise to power. On the right stood a temple to Huitzilopochtli, the god of war. To the left was a similar temple dedicated to Tlaloc, the rain god. The war god brought the Aztec victories that allowed them to enlarge their empire.

The rain god ensured that the land was watered to grow corn and other crops to support the Aztec population.

The ruins fit well with descriptions of the temple left by Spanish chroniclers. They explained that the temples had been painted in bright colors: blood red for the war god, blue for the rain god. They also described a small stone built into the platform on the top of the pyramid. Matos Moctezuma found it still in place, outside the temple of Huitzilopochtli, a couple of yards from the edge of the terrace. This was the stone on which the Aztec killed their prisoners.

▽ A researcher studies a skull found at the Templo Mayor. Bones reveal a lot about how people lived, their age when they died, and even what they ate.

< This codex drawing shows prisoners being killed on a temple pyramid.

off the edge of the pyramid to bounce down to the bottom.

Sacrifice or execution?

Why was the execution of prisoners so important? Scholars working at the Great Temple think that the many deaths might have been a kind of reenactment of the battle between Huitzilopochtli and hi brothers and sister.

Others argue that one of the main reasons the Aztec often went to war with their neighbors was to capture enough prisoners to keep making thei sacrifices to Huitzilopochtli. Unless they kept up their sacrifices, the Aztec believed, their empire would fal

More recently, however, scholars studying the codices have suggested that the trutl maybe more complex—and more ordinary. They argue that all wars have casualtie: whether they are killed in battle or in a temple. The Aztec were simply killing their enemies and saw the

Killing prisoners

The Spaniards were horrified at the spectacle of thousands of prisoners being killed. The monk Bernardino de Sahagún recorded that prisoners lay on their backs over the stone while priests held their arms and legs. Then another priest cut open the victim's chest and pulled out his heart so quickly that it was still beating. The body was rolled

< This figure, called a chacmool, carries a tray to hold the hearts of executed prisoners.

deaths as an extension of the war on the battlefield.

The historians argue that to call the deaths "human sacrifice" makes the Aztec seem unnecessarily cruel. They point out that the accounts of the rituals come from the Spaniards, some of whom saw the Aztec as savages. They also say that the Aztec waged war mainly as a way to increase the amount of tribute paid to the empire. The prisoners were only a secondary consequence of warfare. Nor was all Aztec religion based on blood sacrifice. Aztec homes had shrines to the fire god Xiuhtecuhtli, for example, to whom people made less deadly offerings.

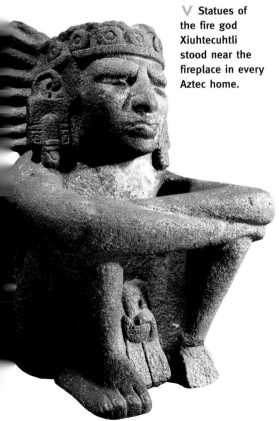

∇ Statues of the fire god Xiuhtecuhtli stood near the fireplace in every Aztec home.

Who can you trust?

The accounts left by Spaniards in Mexico in the 16th century are one of the most important sources of information about the Aztec. But it is important not to forget who wrote them, or how they got their information. Imagine turning up in a place where you do not speak the language and no one speaks yours. You see something you do not understand. How could you find out about it? You might use signs to ask questions and learn answers. If you had enough time, you might be able to learn a few words. Or you might compare what you see to something similar you know from home. That is how most of the Spaniards tried to understand the Aztec. Some archaeologists believe that the Spaniards may have misunderstood ceremonies such as the execution of prisoners. The Spaniards may also have been eager to suggest that the Aztec were savages. It would have made people at home more likely to support the invasion if the troops were acting on behalf of the Christian church to overthrow other religions.

Grip on the imagination

Most scholars continue to believe the traditional view that the Aztec practiced human sacrifice. It is the part of the Aztec story that most fascinates people today. Even people who do not know very much about the Aztec know about the ceremonies in which priests killed thousands of victims on top of the pyramids. That fascination is unlikely to change. But a new way of looking at the killings might eventually help people see the Aztec as something more than bloodthirsty monsters.

CHAPTER 5

A Warrior People

What do we know about Aztec military power?

Hidden in the mountains about 80 miles (130 km) southwest of Tenochtitlan, the stone structures of Malinalco escaped destruction by the Spaniards. The precise purpose of the seven buildings is not known. They stood near the edge of the Aztec Empire. They might have been a frontier outpost. Some clues come from the circular inner chamber of the temple. Inside the doorway, carved in the shape of a serpent's mouth, a low platform curves around

< This ceremonial featherwork shield probably belonged to Ahuitzotl, the eighth Aztec ruler. It depicts a water monster holding a sacrificial knife in its mouth.

AZTEC EMPIRE
ca 1430 – 1521

1100

1600

∧ The temple at Malinalco was carved out of the cliff face in a way that made it look like it had been built from stone blocks.

the wall of a chamber dug out of the cliff face. The platform is carved with a jaguar skin and two eagles; another carved eagle with outstretched wings stands in the center of the floor.

The eagle and the jaguar were important animals for the Aztec. They considered the eagle the greatest hunter in the air and the jaguar the greatest hunter on land. The best soldiers in the Aztec army joined special societies named Eagle Knights and Jaguar Knights. The chamber at Malinalco was probably used in ceremonies to welcome young warriors into these societies. The Aztec emperor sat on a throne carved with a jaguar, so the presence of a carved jaguar might suggest that the emperor himself attended these rituals.

The Aztec's rise to power owed much to their military

< A terra-cotta figure of an Eagle Knight dressed in a costume of eagle-head helmet and feathers.

strength. When they arrived in the Valley of Mexico, they served the Tepanec. The Tepanec were fighting their neighbors, the Colhuacan and the Chichimec of Texcoco. Aztec warriors fought for the Tepanec, but also strengthened their own position. The Aztec grew so important that their leaders married royalty from other cities. When the Tepanec tried to tighten their rule over Tenochtitlan and Texcoco in 1415, the Aztec joined with the Chichimec and another state, Tlacopan, to defeat them.

Rise of the empire

Victory marked the real beginning of the rise of the Aztec. As part of a Triple Alliance with the Chichimec and Tlacopan, they began to build an empire. The Aztec acquired territory through alliances and royal marriages with peoples as far away as Guiengola in the modern state of Oaxaca. But they also fought for power, emerging as skilled warriors.

Warrior knights

The Spaniards recorded that Aztec society was structured to produce warriors. Poets celebrated warfare. Midwives told newborn baby boys of the glory of war. To die in battle, or to be sacrificed as a captive to the gods, meant that the soul would go straight to the afterlife.

Even kings had to prove themselves by military conquest. Carved stones dug up in Mexico City celebrate the victories of two Aztec kings. One, Moctezuma I, was a great general. The other, Tizoc, had much less to celebrate. He lost 300 warriors and took only 40 prisoners. He was a poor general—but tradition said that he still had to have a victory stone. The carvers came up with clever solution. They decorated

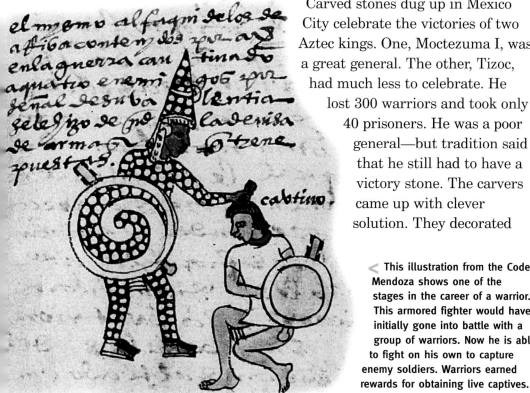

< This illustration from the Codex Mendoza shows one of the stages in the career of a warrior. This armored fighter would have initially gone into battle with a group of warriors. Now he is able to fight on his own to capture enemy soldiers. Warriors earned rewards for obtaining live captives.

Sharing information

How does an archaeologist in Mexico know what an expert studying an Aztec codex in France has discovered? Often there are only a few experts working in a particular field, so they all know each other. They keep in touch by e-mail or share information on the Internet. There are also formal ways to share discoveries. Most experts publish their findings in journals and speak at conferences, where other experts can question their theories. Sometimes a new idea turns out to be weak. Sometimes people who support different theories argue. But at other times archaeologists might hear something that proves to be the missing piece in their own work. For experts to find out as much as possible about the past, it is essential that everyone work together. With the limited clues we have, understanding ancient history is difficult. Sharing information makes things easier.

▽ **Conferences and lectures allow other people to ask questions that may help change or clarify a theory—and make it stronger.**

his stone with scenes from battles that had been fought by other Aztec kings.

Aztec army

Any male over the age of 20 could be drafted to serve in the Aztec army. But there were also professional warriors, who dedicated all their time to warfare. To make sure that men were available to fight, Aztec military operations each year began in late fall, so that the harvest would be over.

Early training

In their first battles, warriors cooperated with other young fighters to capture a prisoner. The captive was killed, and the warriors ritually ate parts of his body. Later, warriors fought on their own, trying to take live captives. A warrior's status grew as he captured more prisoners. When he had captured four, he joined the top rank of soldiers. They were armed with bows and stone-tipped arrows,

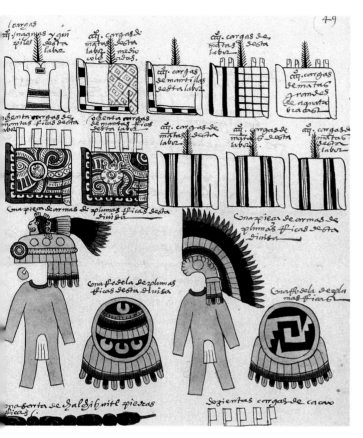

loyalty of the leading warriors, Aztec rulers had to offer them the luxuries that could be obtained only by conquest and tribute. Military heroes wore fine jewels and cloaks that could not be bought anywhere: they were given out only by the emperor himself.

A violent end

The Aztec system was successful—until the Spaniards landed in 1519. Historians have debated the reasons for the sudden downfall of such a mighty empire. Hernán Cortés had a force of only 600 soldiers, but he made alliances with the states defeated by the Aztec.

The Spaniards also had superior weapons, including cannons, and animals the Aztec had never seen: 16 horses. The defeated states saw their chance for revenge and freedom. They were happy to join the Spaniards to try to overthrow their rulers.

lubs whose heads were studded with small pieces of stone, or slings that threw rocks. Warriors also used *tlatls*, hook-shaped throwing devices that could propel a **spear** with great force. The warriors usually tried to take captives without wounding them. An injured captive was no good as an offering to the gods.

Tribute system

Defeated states had to acknowledge Tenochtitlan's power and send food and luxuries to the city. To force other people to pay tribute, the Aztec had to make sure that they were afraid of Tenochtitlan. And to command the

Aztec Daily Life

CHAPTER 6

What was everyday life like in the Aztec Empire?

When Michael E. Smith was a student at Brandeis University in Waltham, Massachusetts, in the 1960s, he kept up to date with the latest archaeological discoveries in Mesoamerica. They all seemed to be spectacular palaces and royal tombs. In museums, he could see luxury items that had been buried with important people. But Smith was puzzled. What about everyone else? He thought that archaeologists were missing a

< This pottery model of an Aztec village shows houses grouped around a central structure that might have been a form of temple.

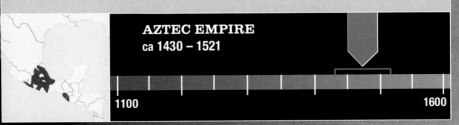

AZTEC EMPIRE
ca 1430 – 1521

1100   1600

▲ This illustration shows two Aztec playing a game called patolli in which players moved counters made from beans around a board.

huge part of the story. The Aztec had ruled as many as 6 million people. How had they lived? No one seemed to know—but Smith wanted to find out.

Pioneering work

As a professor in Chicago, in Albany, New York, and most recently in Arizona, Smith was one of the first experts to investigate Aztec sites outside the great cities and temples. For more than 20 years he has returned to Mexico every year with his wife, archaeologist Cynthia Heath-Smith, and their daughters.

Smith concentrated on the modern state of Morelos. The Aztec ruins there had not been investigated and had not been damaged by later building. The region had been home to the Tlahuica, subjects of the Aztec in Tenochtitlan.

Smith concentrated on the town of Yautepec and two smaller sites: Capilco, a village of just 21 homes, and Cuexcomate, which had more than 150 homes, temples, and storerooms.

Feeding the empire

At each site, Smith randomly chose houses to excavate. His team found a number of clues. The most useful were broken bits of pottery. The style of pottery changed over time, so Smith could date the pieces by comparing them to finds at other Aztec sites. He worked out that the settlements had been occupied from about 1200 to 1550. In the late 1400s, both sites had grown quickly. If the population had increased so rapidly across the whole of the region, Smith decided, there would have been too many people to feed.

Secrets from plants

When Michael Smith explored fields in Morelos, he wanted to learn what crops the Tlahuica grew. One of the techniques he used was pollen analysis, which he hoped would identify grains found in soil behind old dams. Pollen analysis is a type of archaeology in which tiny spores and grains are used to analyze what plants grew where and when. Every plant species has different pollen (hibiscus, *magnified below*), so it is useful for identification. The other great thing for experts is that pollen does not decay. Smith's samples turned out not to give any clear results. But pollen analysis remains an important tool, especially when used together with other methods to understand an ancient environment.

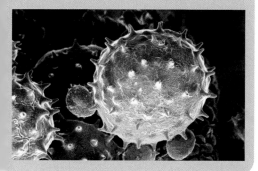

Farmers would have had to use new methods to grow more food.

In the hills nearby, Smith found evidence that the Aztec had indeed learned to increase the amount of land for crops. They had built walls to support terraces, steps of flat land cut into the hillsides, and dams to block streams. When rain washed soil off the hillsides into the streams, the dams trapped particles of soil carried in the water. This soil eventually formed a patch of land for more crops.

At home with the Aztec

The rural Tlahuica farmers and their families lived in small, one-room homes. The houses had walls made of *adobe*, mud shaped into bricks and dried in the sun. The roofs were likely made out of thatch. Each house had two doors, but probably no windows. Smith suggests that people spent a lot of time outdoors. The houses were grouped around small courtyards,

∨ A bowl and two cups for drinking pulque, an alcoholic drink. Such high-quality, decorated pottery was probably used by nobles or priests.

which probably provided space for chores such as preparing food. The Spaniards said that most Aztec households had five or six members. Sometimes all the residents in a courtyard belonged to the same large family.

Marvelous middens

More clues lay in the trash. Outside each house, the inhabitants tossed their trash onto heaps that archaeologists call *middens*. Every time Smith excavated a home, he also dug a pit into its trash heap. He found broken objects such as cooking pots and blades made of obsidian.

Smith found thousands of pieces of pottery. The Spaniards had reported that so much broken pottery gathered around houses and yards that children used the pieces as toys.

The remains Smith found in the middens included tools used to grind corn into flour, and flat griddles that were used to cook tortillas.

There were also pots used to cook beans, which were the other big part of the diet.

The same basic ingredients and ways of cooking were still at the heart of the fiestas villagers held for Smith

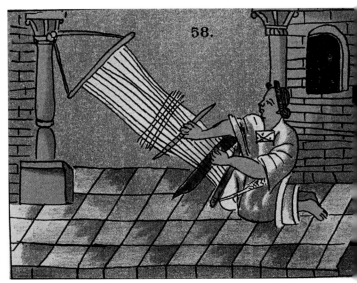

∧ This panel from a codex shows a woman weaving. Almost all Aztec households produced their own textiles.

< The Aztec used this vessel in the shape of a hare for drinking cocoa, which they believed was good for their health.

and his colleagues at the end of each digging season. The Mexican food that is popular around the world today is very similar to what the Aztec enjoyed five hundred years ago. The only major change to Mexican cooking is the addition of ingredients introduced by Europeans, such as wheat.

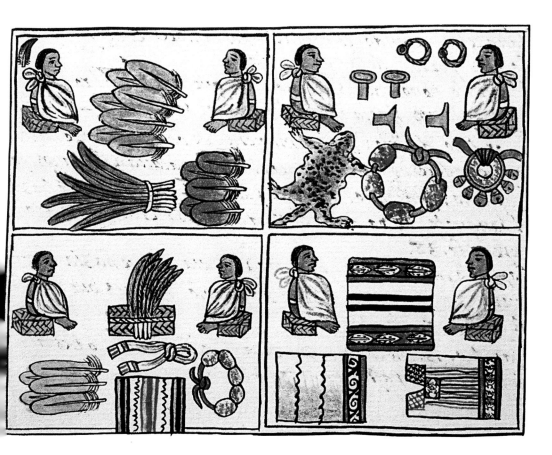

Textiles and tree bark

apilco and Cuexcomate were a long way from the heart of the empire. ut Smith discovered that their citizens were surprisingly well off. In every house, he found spindles, weights, and bowls. They were used in the process of spinning cotton into fibers that could be woven into textiles on looms. Some homes also had bronze needles for sewing. Textile making was probably done by women while men worked in the fields.

The woven textiles were traded a market in return for goods such as salt and painted pottery. Such goods

▲ This codex illustration shows a market where merchants display a wide range of goods, including carpets, feathers, and animal fur.

were sometimes imported over quite long distances. Salt came from the Valley of Mexico, for example, and bronze from western Mexico. Pachuca and Otumba were important sources of obsidian.

Another important item for trade was paper. It was used to produce the Aztec's codices. In some houses, Smith discovered tools that were used to beat tree bark into thin sheets to make paper. He also found traces of paints that were produced for artists to color the codices.

∧ Michael Smith's team found a collection of household gods during an excavation.

Tribute and trade

Paper was one of the most important parts of the tribute that the Tlahuica paid to the empire. But even though they had to send goods to the Aztec, the farmers of Morelos were able to produce enough crops and other goods not only to pay the tribute but also to trade for themselves.

Smith's work is filling in gaps in what we know about Aztec life and confirming other accounts. The Spanish leader Hernán Cortés had recorded in wonder the range of goods on sale in the markets in Tlatelolco, the sister city of Tenochtitlan. He was amazed by the bright spun cotton and pigment for painters—there was far more choice of color than at home in Spain. Most people traded using beans or small copper axe blades for money.

A special class of merchants, called *pochteca*, traded with what the Aztec

called the Hot Lands. They traveled in caravans as far south as today's Panama. Their journeys could last years, with porters carrying loads 30 or 40 miles (48–65 km) a day. The merchants brought home green jade, shells of tortoises and other sea creatures, jaguar skins, and bright bird feathers—luxury goods for the rulers of the empire.

> Craftsmen make headdresses for sale or to send as tribute to Tenochtitlan.

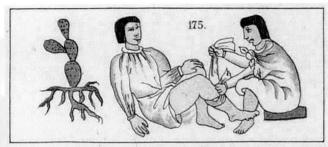

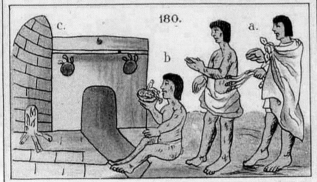

< These Aztec illustrations show healers looking after patients with different problems, including an injured leg *(top)* and fleas *(middle)*.

held positions of authority; they could even own slaves themselves.

Magnificent medicine

Among the most important groups in Aztec society were healers. In 1991, when Pope John Paul II visited Mexico, he returned the earliest American medical book. The Badianus Manuscript was written in 1552 by the Aztec physician Martinus de la Cruz. It was translated into Latin and sent to the Spanish king Charles V. It later passed to the Vatican Library.

The codex contained illustrated recipes for herbal remedies. Aztec medicine was partly based on the intervention of gods and goddesses, but it also relied on a deep knowledge of roots, herbs, and other natural substances. The drawings in the codex show which parts of herbs to use in different cures. Experts studying the manuscript have learned that in medicine—as in other areas of daily life such as education—the Aztec were far more advanced than their European contemporaries.

Social structure

The rulers were at the top of a society that was divided into clear ranks. Among the most important were the warriors, priests, and officials who ran the empire. The vast majority of the population were peasant farmers. There were also many slaves. Some became slaves as punishment for a crime, but most sold themselves to earn money for their family or to get themselves out of debt. Slaves often

Meet an Archaeologist

Michael E. Smith is a professor at Arizona State University. He was a pioneer in excavating rural sites in Mexico to find out how ordinary Aztec lived. His digs in Morelos have revealed much about daily life.

What made you want to be an archaeologist?

I didn't know much about archaeology when I was young, but one of my favorite places to play was in the ruined foundation of an old mansion in some woods near my house. I wondered what it had looked like, who had lived there, and why they had left so many things in the dirt around the house. I still have a fascination with ruins, and I still ask these same questions about the sites I excavate.

Why did you decide to focus on rural life rather than the Aztec cities?

After I completed my Ph.D., I realized that very little was known about Aztec peasants or the countryside. Two sites had recently been found (Cuexcomate and Capilco) that had good potential for learning about Aztec rural life. No one was working on that topic, and it seemed I could make a real contribution.

Later I realized that Aztec cities were also very poorly understood, and I moved my fieldwork to urban sites. But I still focused on the everyday lives of people, studied through the excavation of houses.

Why is it important to know about ordinary people?

Too many studies in archaeology have focused on palaces, temples, and tombs. These buildings give us information about kings, nobles, and the upper classes. In ancient societies, however, these upper classes are less than 5 percent of the population. If we really want to know something about ancient societies, we shouldn't ignore 95 percent of the people. Tombs, palaces, and fancy jewelry are important clues, but they don't tell the whole story about an ancient people.

What's the best part of your job?

The best part of the job is excavation—uncovering the houses, farms, and places where people once lived and worked. It's exciting when the diggers first find a wall or floor or other feature buried under the ground. Then we have to clear off the remains and try to find artifacts that go with the building. Often the artifacts give us the best information about ancient people and their lives.

Q What's the worst part of your job?
A Two things. The first is the delay between excavation and being able to interpret and understand the site. Since one month of excavation requires several more months to classify and study the artifacts, and since we can usually go to Mexico to work only in the summer, it takes years to get all of the results completed. The second unpleasant aspect is the work necessary to get a project going. We must apply for funding and excavation permits as well as convince landowners to let us dig on their property. These things take up a lot of time that I would rather spend doing fieldwork or artifact analysis.

Q What are the most important qualities for an archaeologist?
A Patience, intelligence, a strong curiosity about the world, perseverance, creativity, and a love of the outdoors.

Q Is there much left to learn about the Aztec?

∧ Michael E. Smith shares some finds with Mexican schoolchildren.

A There is an incredible amount that we still do not know about the Aztec. In comparison to the Greeks or Egyptians, we know next to nothing about them. Although newly discovered documents will provide some information, most new knowledge will come from archaeology.

Q What was your most important discovery?
A Those of us who study ancient houses and commoners rarely make a "discovery" comparable to unearthing a royal tomb. I did discover that Aztec peasants had tools and jewelry of copper and bronze in their houses, which shows that they had access to valuable imported goods. It also shows that these objects were traded across the hostile border between the Aztec and Tarascan empires.

Q What are the biggest challenges for working in Mexico?
A Mexico has a huge number of sites and it is impossible to protect or study all of them. The population is growing, cities are expanding, and these processes bring great damage to ancient cities. It is a real challenge for governments and for archaeologists to learn as much as we can about the ancient past before the sites are damaged or destroyed.

A Recovered Past

CHAPTER 7

What is still left to learn about the peoples from Mexico's past?

The destruction of the Aztec civilization began almost as soon as the Spaniards arrived in Mexico. Cortés and his men wanted to replace Aztec beliefs with their own. They smashed hundreds of statues and destroyed old codices, but that was nothing compared to the damage they caused in other ways. Unknown to the troops and the settlers who arrived later, they carried diseases that had never existed in the Americas. The Aztec had no natural defense against these diseases. Hundreds of thousands of

< Mexicans wearing Aztec costume parade in Mexico City in 2006. Many Mexicans are proud of their Aztec past, even though most of them now also have some European ancestors.

people—maybe millions—died from illnesses such as smallpox.

Yet the Spaniards did not wipe out all traces of the Aztec. Today more than 1.6 million Mexicans still speak a form of the Aztec's Nahuatl language. Many peasants still live in ways that resemble the lives of their Aztec ancestors. They grow similar crops in the same fields and make the same dishes such as corn tortillas and beans. The vast majority of Mexicans are mestizos, who combine European

∧ A Mexican and his daugher make a carnival mask based on the Aztec god Quetzalcoatl.

and Aztec descent. For many, the idea of the Aztec has become very important as a way to take pride in their mixed roots.

The Aztec are also an important symbol for Mexican-Americans, or Chicanos, in the United States. In the late 1960s, a Chicano civil rights movement was inspired by Aztlan, the mythical homeland of the Aztec. Some people tried to find Aztlan in the southwestern United States. For others, Aztlan was more important simply as an idea that linked their past to both the American Southwest and ancient Mexico.

Building with the past

When it comes to physical remains, too, the Aztec legacy did not vanish altogether. In Cuernavaca, for example, Cortés built a house directly on top of the palace of the local king. The palace vanished for more than four hundred years, but today its ruins are visible again. They were found during construction in the early 1970s. The builders changed their plans to leave the old walls on display. Other architects have also changed their plans when they find old ruins.

But not everyone is so interested in the past. A builder told archaeologist Augusto F. Molina Montes how he once uncovered an Aztec war canoe while digging some foundations. Rather than face a delay while experts examined the find, he

> Floodlights light up the sky above the Zocalo to celebrate the millennium in January 2000—above the ruins of the temple built more than 500 years earlier.

quickly buried the canoe again—and kept working.

New discoveries are still being made—and many are important ones. As this book shows, there have been breakthroughs since the start of the 21st century. Even at the Templo Mayor in Mexico City, one of the most investigated of all Aztec sites, there may still be important things left to discover.

Acid rain

In 2007 pollution expert Humberto Bravo reported that ancient carvings were being eaten away at an alarming rate by acid rain. The site at El Tajin, on the Gulf Coast, is near oil platforms and power plants. Bravo believes that chemicals released into the air are mixing with rain to create a powerful acid. El Tajin was built by the Totonac people before the Aztec arrived in Mexico. It is famous for its pyramid and its carvings of people playing a ball game. Now, Bravo says, they are both under threat unless the pollution can be stopped.

Archaeology is big business in Mexico. Millions of tourists visit the great sites such as Teotihuacan every year. The National Museum of Anthropology in Mexico City is one of the world's most important museums. Visitors examine the huge collections of objects from the Aztec and earlier peoples. Many are Mexicans who are interested in their own past; others have come from all over the world. They all want to learn more about the fascinating story of the Aztec: how a small group of warriors, traders, and farmers built one of the greatest empires the world has ever seen.

The Years Ahead

This is an exciting time to be an archaeologist in Mexico. After decades of studying mainly written sources, people are excavating more ancient sites and making new finds. Mexican scholars from the National Institute of History and Anthropology are taking the lead, but archaeologists from all over the world want to work in Mexico.

There are still problems, however. One of the main troubles is money. Archaeology is slow and expensive. So many ancient artifacts are turning up in Mexico that it is impossible to process them all. Michael Smith's digs in Morelos, for example, have revealed so many finds that it is difficult to know what to do with them. The law prevents them from being removed from the country, but the Mexican government has other priorities for spending its money than on new museums. In some cases, Smith's team has had to record finds and rebury them to await analysis. Smith hopes to find money to build a warehouse to keep all of the evidence he has found.

In the meantime, work goes on and new objects appear. Many add to our understanding of the Aztec—but some raise new questions. There is still much to be discovered about Mexico's fascinating past.

⋀ Excavations are going on all the time in Mexico; these archaeologists are working in Mexico City in 2005

Glossary

adobe – a brick made of dried earth and straw

aqueduct – a pipeline or channel used to transport water, often over long distances

architect – a person who designs buildings or gives advice on their construction

artifact – any object changed by human activity

bioarchaeologist – an archaeologist who studies the history of living things

carbon – an element found in all living things; it can be used to date objects accurately

causeway – a narrow roadway across water such as a lake

ceramics – objects made from clay

chronicle – a record of historical events, written as they occurred

circa – about; used to indicate a date that is approximate and abbreviated as ca

conquistador – a leader or soldier in the Spanish conquest of Central and South America

excavation – an archaeological dig

foundations – the buried base that supports a building

idol – a statue of a god used in religious ceremonies

imperial – something associated with an empire or emperor

jaguar – a large wildcat found mostly in central and South America

lament – a sad song in memory of something that has been lost or someone who has died

luxuries – expensive objects that give pleasure to their owners but are not necessary for everyday life

Mesoamerica – Middle America; a term used to describe an area from central Mexico south through Guatemala, Belize, Honduras, and El Salvador

Nahuatl – the language of the ancient Aztec

omens – signs that people believe can be used to tell the future

piles – long columns of wood, steel, or concrete that are driven into the ground to support a building

pollen – tiny particles that are produced by plants

preconquest – dating from before the Spaniards landed in Mexico in 1519

provisions – food and other supplies that are necessary for everyday life

pyramid – a building with a square base that rises to a point

rituals – repeated practices that relate to specific, often religious, ceremonies

shards – broken pieces of pottery

summit – the highest point

terra-cotta – a form of clay that is often a red-brown color; the color is also known as terra-cotta

textiles – woven cloth

theory – in science, the explanation that best accounts for all of the known facts

tribute – payments made by a weaker state to a stronger state, either as money or as goods

urban – belonging to a city

Bibliography

Books

Aztecs: Reign of Blood and Splendor. Alexandria, VA: Time-Life Books, 1992.

Baquedano, Elizabeth. *Aztec, Inca & Maya.* New York: Dorling Kindersley, 1993.

Coe, Michael D. *Mexico: From the Olmecs to the Aztecs.* New York: Thames and Hudson, 2002.

Smith, Michael E. *The Aztecs* (Peoples of America). Malden, MA: Blackwell, 2002.

Articles

McDowell, Bart. "The Aztecs." NATIONAL GEOGRAPHIC (December 1980): 714–751.

Matos Moctezuma, Eduardo. "New Finds in the Great Temple." NATIONAL GEOGRAPHIC (December 1980): 667–775.

Molina Montes, Augusto F. "The Building of Tenochtitlan." NATIONAL GEOGRAPHIC (December 1980): 753–765.

Wilkerson, S. Jeffrey J. "Following Cortés: Path to Conquest." NATIONAL GEOGRAPHIC (October 1984): 420–459.

Further Reading

Pohl, John. *Aztec Warrior: A.D. 1325–1521* (Warrior). Oxford: Osprey Publishing, 2001.

Ramen, Fred. *Hernán Cortés: The Conquest of Mexico and the Aztec Empire* (Library of Explorers and Exploration). New York: Rosen Publishing Group, 2003.

Sonneborn, Liz. *The Ancient Aztecs* (People of the Ancient World). New York: Franklin Watts, 2005.

On the Web

ThinkQuest Aztec site
http://library.thinkquest.org/27981/

Templo Mayor Museum
http://archaeology.la.asu.edu/tm/index2.php

Michael E. Smith Homepage and Excavations Blog
http://www.public.asu.edu/~mesmith9/

UNESCO World Heritage List for Mexico
http://whc.unesco.org/en/statesparties/mx

About the Author

TIM COOKE is a graduate of Oxford University. He has worked in children's publishing for more than 20 years as an author and editor, and has contributed to dozens of encyclopedias on a wide range of subjects. He has traveled to Mexico a number of times and says that visiting the Templo Mayor in the heart of Mexico City is a strange experience for anyone used to ancient ruins being quiet and isolated.

About the Consultant

ELIZABETH GRAHAM earned a Ph.D. in archaeology from Cambridge University before becoming a lecturer in Mesoamerican archaeology at University College, London. She has written widely about the Aztec.

Sources for Quotations

Page 21: Williams, A.R. "Mexico's Pyramid of Death." NATIONAL GEOGRAPHIC (October 2006): 144-153.
Page 31: Quoted in *Aztecs: Reign of Blood and Splendor*, Time-Life Books, 1992.

> Aztec mask made from small pieces of turquoise.

One of the world's largest nonprofit scientific and educational organizations, the National Geographic Society was founded in 1888 "for the increase and diffusion of geographic knowledge." Fulfilling this mission, the Society educates and inspires millions every day through its magazines, books, television programs, videos, maps and atlases, research grants, the National Geographic Bee, teacher workshops, and innovative classroom materials. The Society is supported through membership dues, charitable gifts, and income from the sale of its educational products. This support is vital to National Geographic's mission to increase global understanding and promote conservation of our planet through exploration, research, and education.

For more information, please call 1-800-NGS-LINE (647-5463) or write to the following address:

National Geographic Society
1145 17th Street N.W.
Washington, D.C. 20036-4688
U.S.A.

Visit the Society's Web site:
www.nationalgeographic.com

Library of Congress Cataloging-in-Publication Data available upon request
Hardcover ISBN: 978-1-4263-0072-1
Library Edition ISBN: 978-1-4263-0073-8

Printed in Mexico

Series design by Jim Hiscott
The body text is set in Century Schoolbook
The display text is set in Helvetica Neue, Clarendon

National Geographic Society

John M. Fahey, Jr., *President and Chief Executive Officer;* Gilbert M. Grosvenor, *Chairman of the Board;* Nina D. Hoffman, Executive Vice President, *President of Book Publishing Group*

Staff for This Book

Nancy Laties Feresten, *Vice President, Editor-in-Chief of Children's Books*
Virginia Ann Koeth, *Project Editor*
Bea Jackson, *Director of Design and Illustration*
David M. Seager, *Art Director*
Lori Epstein, National Geographic Image Sales, *Illustrations Editors*
Jean Cantu, *Illustrations Specialist*
Carl Mehler, *Director of Maps*
Priyanka Lamichhane, *Assistant Editor*

R. Gary Colbert, *Production Director*
Lewis R. Bassford, *Production Manager*
Maryclare Tracy, Nicole Elliott, *Manufacturing Managers*

For the Brown Reference Group, plc

Emily Hill, *Editor*
Alan Gooch, *Book Designer*

Photo Credits

Front: © Dagli Orti/Museo del Templo Mayor Mexico/The Art Archives
Back: © The British Museum, London/Werner Forman Archives
Spine: © James Bramwell/Shutterstock; Icon: © Tomasz Otap/Shutterstock

NGIC = National Geographic Image Collection; WFA = Werner Forman Archives; AA = The Art Archives
1, © The British Museum, London/WFA; 2-3, © Martin Grey/NGIC; 4, © Gianni Dagli Orti/Corbis; 6, © Charles & Josette Lenars/Corbis; 9, © Elizabeth Graham; 10 left, © Private Collection/WFA; 10 right, © National Museum of Anthropology, Mexico/WFA; 11 top, © P. Goldman Collection/WFA; 11 bottom, © National Museum of Anthropology, Mexico/ WFA; 12–13, © Daniel Aguilar/ Reuters/Corbis; 14, © Eduardo Verdugo/ AP/Empics; 15 top © National Museum of Anthropology, Mexico/WFA; 15 bottom, © Mexicolore/ Museo Nacional de Antropologia, Mexico/Ian Mursell/ Bridgeman Art Library; 16, © Pigorini Museum of Prehistory & Ethnography/WFA; 17, © WFA; 18–19, © Kenneth Garrett/NGIC; 20 center, © Jack Unruh/ NGIC; 20 bottom, © Jesus Eduardo Lopez Reyes/NGIC; 21 center, Kenneth Garrett/NGIC; 21 bottom, © National Museum of Anthropology, Mexico/WFA; 22, © Robert Knight/Eye Ubiquitous/ Hutchison; 23 top, © Anthropology Museum, Veracruz University, Jalapa/ WFA; 23 bottom, © Kenneth Garrett/NGIC; 24–25, © Dagli Orti/AA; 26, © Gianni Dagli Orti/Corbis; 27, © WFA; 28 top, © National Museum of Anthropology, Mexico/WFA; 28 bottom, © John Berkey/NGIC; 29, © Charles & Josette Lenars/Corbis; 30, © National Museum of Anthropology, Mexico/WFA; 31, © Giraudon/ Bridgeman Art Library; 32–33, © KD/ Keystone USA/Rex Features; 34, © Gianni Dagli Orti/ Corbis; 35, © Keith Dannemiller/Corbis; 36 top © AA; 36 bottom, © N. J. Saunders/WFA; 37, © The British Museum, London/WFA; 38-39, © Museum fur Volkerkunde Vienna/WFA; 40 top, © Dagli Orti/AA; 40 bottom, © Dagli Orti/AA; 41, © Bodleian Library, Oxford/AA; 42, © A. Huber/U. Starke/Zefa/ Corbis; 43, © Bodleian Library, Oxford/AA; 44–45, © Richard A. Cooke/Corbis; 46, © Dagli Orti/AA; 47 center, © Jim Zuckerman/ Corbis; 47 bottom, © The British Museum, London/ WFA; 48 top, © Mireille Vautier/AA; 48 bottom, © National Museum of Anthropology, Mexico/WFA; 49 top, © Michael E. Smith; 49 bottom, © Templo Mayor Library, Mexico/Dagli Orti/AA; 50 top, © Michael E. Smith; 50 bottom, © Mireille Vautier/AA; 51, © AA; 52 © Michael E. Smith; 53 © Michael E. Smith; 54-55, © Marco Ugarte/AP/Empics; 56, © Tomasz Tomaszewski/ NGIC; 57, © Antonia Clasos/Sygma/Corbis; 58, © Daniel Aguilar/Reuters/Corbis; 63, © The British Museum, London/Werner Forman.

Front cover: A detail from a ceramic vase representing the rain god, Tlaloc
Page 1 and back cover: Pectoral ornament in the form of a double-headed serpent, meant to be worn by a high priest
Pages 2–3: Mt. Iztaccihuatl rises in the distance. The name means "Sleeping Lady" or "White Lady" in Nau hatt, the language of the Aztec.